CRITICAL LEADERSHIFT

why traditional management techniques are
counter-productive in the modern workplace

…and what you can do to turn things around

SARA CHRISTIANSEN

Critical Leadershift

Edited by: Travis Theurer

Sara Christiansen
CEO and VP of Client Services
www.ideation-consulting.com
sarada@ideation-consulting.com
507-217-9767

Printed in the United States of America
Second Printing January 2014
ISBN-13 9781489543226
LCCN

0   9   8   7   6   5   4   3   2

I would like to dedicate this book in memoriam to Sandra Rademacher. Although we met only a few short years before you were called home, I will always treasure the time we worked together. Your counsel and friendship opened up amazing opportunities for me.

Thank you my friend.

Contents

TOO IMPORTANT TO FAIL

Social Media has had an enormous impact on our society and the world culture. Entire governments have fallen due to revolutionary movements that evolved on Twitter and Facebook. Global policies and individual beliefs alike are being shaped by the publically posted thoughts of persons we may have never met (or haven't been in the same room with since Mr. Pezetti's sophomore algebra class). And, although there are many fascinating implications of social media to consider, I want to focus on one phenomenon that has caught the attention of this passionate Social Scientist.

I joined Facebook back in 2008. Early on I realized that this medium would change our collective existence. We can now articulate our most intimate thoughts and feelings to an audience as large as our network of "on-line friends" can reach. I can share my everyday occurrences, as well as major life events, with friends, family and strangers across the globe in mere seconds. And, they can reply back to describe their thoughts and feelings about my thoughts and feelings.

However, lately, I have become gravely concerned about the reoccurring theme to the posts of my network on Sunday evenings.

Every Sunday around suppertime, people that I deeply care about (or at least remember fondly) are posting about their sincere dread to return to their miserable jobs, with their horrible bosses and loathsome co-workers, the next day. My news feed page often lights up with posts describing the horror to come on Monday morning as the weekend concludes and the workweek begins. I have read about sick days taken for fabricated illnesses, long awaited *mental health* days and fantasies of leaving the "rat race" all together.

Although some of these posts can be quite humorous, I am very distressed by the underlying implications of this rampant disdain for the workplace. The average American worker will spend more than 80,000 hours of their life at work. The only thing we do more is *sleep*. So, it saddens me to think that so many of us are spending the majority of our hours on this earth in pure misery. Why do we accept that the experience of earning a living has to be so torturous?

Can't we find a better way?

And to further complicate this issue, study after study has proven that prolonged workplace stress and anxiety has a predominately negative impact on our health and may actually shorten our life expectancy. We clearly understand that high stress can lead to gastro-intestinal complications, hypertension, headaches, chemical abuse, mental health concerns, sleep disorders and many other serious health implications. But, did you realize that prolonged stress and anxiety has been proven to have a significantly negative impact on *job performance*?

Workplace stress imparts serious limitations on creativity, memory, analytical capabilities, patience and concentration. Highly stressed employees tend to report greater difficulty communicating effectively, maintaining quality inter-personal relationships and solving problems.

So, as we are still struggling to recover from the recent economic downturn, I assert that we can no longer afford to accept that a vast number of American workers are so miserable on the job. This not only causes long-ranging health concerns, the fact we are not as productive as we possibly could be greatly limits our nation's recovery efforts and competitive advantage. Therefore, I declare that we are squarely in the midst of a *Great American Workplace Crisis*.

We all agree that leadership is the pivotal key to success or failure in every workplace. Without effective leadership, no organization can realize its highest potential. So, if we are to change the experience of working to that which promotes health, performance and productivity, then we must first consider how to change our methods of leadership.

I have worked with countless leaders over the last decade, and I find that these folks typically have three major accountabilities:

Functional duties: the day-to-day technical work; (e.g., production, customer service, maintenance, etc.)

Administrative duties: the internal processes that keep the business running smoothly; (e.g., payroll, report generation, accounting, etc.)

Managerial duties: improving the performance of employees; (e.g., training, motivation, coaching, etc.)

Take a moment to think about your job. Over the last week, how have you spent your time? List the major tasks you worked on and the hours you have invested in each line item. Then, go back and review your list. Decide which category (functional, administrative or managerial) best describes each task.

If you are like most leaders I meet, the time spent performing functional and administrative tasks long outweighs the amount of time invested in managerial duties. I have discovered there are a number of reasons why this happens.

First, most leaders will focus on the tasks that they are generally held most accountable for. So, if someone is constantly asking you how production is going - or if you have completed your monthly reports - these are the activities you will view as the greatest priority.

Second, functional and administrative duties typically have a start and a finish. It feels good to cross tasks off of our to-do lists, and we are often rewarded for meeting specific deadlines.

The problem is: Managerial duties rarely land at the top of our priority lists. Training, motivating and coaching employees does not have a deadline, we can't cross it off our to-do list (because the job is never truly finished), and we are rarely held accountable for these (as one general manager I was coaching a few years ago so eloquently put it) "fluffy" kind of tasks.

But, if you stop and ask yourself to define what it means to be a leader, I think you will be surprised by your answer. So, let's explore...

Why do we need leaders/managers?

When I ask this question of leaders that I am coaching, I often hear statements like, "I am responsible to keep everyone focused," or, "I need to ensure we are working as a team," and "to make sure everyone is meeting their goals." These are all outcomes that require a dedication to our managerial duties because the primary responsibility of a manger is *driving results through people*.

Or, in modern human resource terms: *performance management*.

Now, I know that when most of you hear the term performance management you probably cringe and your face starts to scrunch up in agony.

But wait! I propose that we look at performance management through a new lens.

Most managers and HR professionals associate the responsibility of performance management with the dreaded *annual review*. I have yet to find a manager, or employee, that actually looks forward to that magical time of year that requires us to fill out the form (you know the one that HR has sweated over updating for the last 12 months), solicit feedback (can you say 360 @#$$%), and have a conversation to discuss all the areas in which we "need improvement."

No wonder you are cringing!

However, all of the current research being done clearly proves that most of our traditional management practices actually have a negative (yes, I said *negative*) impact on performance. It seems that we are ensuring the opposite of the one thing we are trying to achieve: *improved performance.*

Astonishingly, most of the managerial methods that we wager our organizational success upon originated in the early 1900s.

Frederick Winslow Taylor, who is commonly known as the father of modern management, authored the book *The Principles of Scientific Management* in 1911. The premise of his work was based upon his belief that the common American worker was uneducated, unskilled and stupid.

Although I doubt that our recent ancestors were less intelligent than us, Taylor was accurate in the fact that the average worker of the time had rarely completed the eighth grade and possessed scarcely few specialized occupational skills.

Taylor, therefore, strategized that management needs to closely monitor and supervise each and every worker. From this philosophy, we have garnered most of the management techniques (including the *annual review*) that we depend on still today.

For example, the *job description* is an antiquated tool that is held sacred in most workplaces. Managers and HR professionals spend endless hours creating, editing and updating these complex documents. For what? To be handed out at new hire orientation and promptly thrown in the bottom desk drawer?

Who among you has recently reviewed your job description? Be honest. I thought not.

Job descriptions are no longer adequate. I am not saying throw them all out. (Well, you can if you want.) But, I am asking you to no longer rely on this one document to communicate expectations to employees.

Jobs today (unlike in Taylor's era) are complex, ever-changing, and market driven. If you were to create a truly comprehensive job description, the document would be 25+ pages, you would have to update it daily, and it would still wind up in the bottom desk drawer.

What about the *40-hour work week*?

This staple of the workplace was first instituted by Harry S. Truman. The concept originated in a time when most work was mechanical in nature and having a job meant that your employer was essentially renting your hands and feet by the hour. This is no longer the case.

The modern workplace demands that employees be creative and adaptable, solve problems, troubleshoot, serve customer needs, work as a team, identify and leverage opportunities - all of which requires intellect. How much intellect can you produce in an hour? In a week?

What about *progressive discipline*?

You know: The practice of issuing a verbal, then a written and, ultimately, a final warning before you terminate a problem employee. This practice was actually developed in the 1930s by the unions. Their intent was to prevent (or postpone) the loss of work for the rank and file.

Today, we depend on this warning issuance system as our first line of defense. Many truly believe that this ritual will actually turn around our employees' poor performance. The problem is that it rarely (if ever) works. It does however, postpone the inevitable. But, while you are going through the motions (which usually takes at least 90 days), you have sent a message to the rest of your team that it takes three strikes before you will really address a problem, thereby diminishing the overall productivity of the entire team.

I have never witnessed (I am not saying it has never happened, I am just saying I have yet to see) someone who has received a final warning and then suddenly become a valued employee.

And, what about the *chain of command?*

The concept of a chain of command, and the ever present organizational chart, can be traced back to the civil war. Usually an intricate diagram of solid and dotted lines, we still use this structure to govern decision-making, authority and pay ranges. In contrast, however, I routinely see this practice erode creativity, initiative, empowerment and morale.

All good leaders understand that their role is a critically important one. And, you now know that this importance transcends many of the commonly held wisdoms.

Being a good leader goes far beyond being the final decision maker, or the rule setter, or the raise giver, or the terminator, or the task assigner, or the performance evaluator. You now know that being a good leader is about helping each individual improve their performance, so the team will achieve greater success.

And, you now know that in order to do that effectively we need a new perspective, a LEADER*SHIFT*.

"The people who are crazy enough to believe that they can change the world are the ones who do."

-Apple Computers, 1997

THE BALANCED PLAYBOOK

When company leaders are considering large capital purchases - like a new enterprise system, or upgraded equipment, or a facility expansion, or research and development of a new product line, or mergers and acquisitions - they are wise to spend a considerable amount of time and effort determining the financial *return on this investment*. This method is commonly referred to as analyzing the *ROI*.

Effective leaders know that if the return does not outweigh the investment within a reasonable amount of time then it is not a smart move.

Companies are constantly stating, "Our employees are our greatest asset," but what does this mean?

I encourage you to take out your current budget. Now take a look at the line items in the liability (costs) section. If your company is like most organizations, employee wages and benefits top the list. And, this number is likely to increase year after year. This proves that employees are technically more of a *liability* than an *asset*, right?

Not necessarily. Employees actually become an *asset* when we can quantify their *VALUE* - the extent to which an employee's contributions exceed (or fail to equal) the investment made in their employment.

So what is the ROI on your organization's biggest investment, your employees? If you do not know, you are not alone.

The answer lies in your definition of *PERFORMANCE.*

When I talk with leaders and HR professionals, I often ask them how they define good performance in their organizations. All too often I hear tales about perfect attendance, or policy adherence, or folks that quietly do their work and don't cause any trouble.

While I agree that it is important for employees to be punctual, follow rules and not stir up too much conflict, I do not agree that this is a good definition of *performance.* I assert that these (along with a set of designated job duties) are the minimum requirements for continued employment.

If an employee is only accomplishing enough to avoid getting fired, I hope that they are not considered to be a *good performer.*

Most managers today believe their toughest responsibility is keeping employees *in line.* For me, this conjures up an image liken to the first grade when we were all asked to line up by the classroom door (in alphabetical order) and proceed to the lunch room every day. (My maiden name is

Gabel, so I was always in the middle; never the front nor the back.) However, keeping folks *in-line* means that your managers are spending a great deal of time and effort focusing on making sure that employees aren't falling behind your *minimum* expectations.

Can this be the formula for success?

Let's compare the common workplace to a professional football team.

If you are a coach in the NFL and you want to be highly successful, your goals are likely to be set squarely on winning the Super Bowl. This is a clear definition of success. Also, you probably further define performance as *repeatedly scoring **more** points (and therefore winning **more** games) than your opponents.* Therefore, it is your responsibility to develop a game plan that includes a balanced focus on good defense and a positive offense.

Your offensive plays must be effective at moving the ball down the field and into the end zone, while your defensive strategies must prevent your opponents from doing the same.

If you have a great offense and a not-so-great defense, you have a good chance of scoring a lot of points, but so does your opponent. If you have a wonderful defense and a lousy offense, the best you can hope for is a 0-0 tie.

How can this be a winning strategy?

The same is true in the workplace. If leaders in your organization are spending the majority of their time and effort making sure that rules are not broken and mistakes are not being made, the best you can do is to *not get any worse*.

Can't you just hear the cheerleaders chanting, "We don't suck! We don't suck!"?

Developing a balanced playbook is often a difficult mind shift for most managers. The business world (and your own well-meaning HR team) has been telling you for years that the #1 priority for a manager is to instill compliance throughout your team. You have been programmed to focus on ensuring that the rules and policies are followed by each and every employee. You have likely been told that if there is any hint of impropriety, you will inevitably find yourself facing a judge during an ugly lawsuit.

Most leaders learned long ago that it is in their best interest to follow a compliance-driven management model. And this has become a widely held definition of *good* leadership.

In every situation managers tend to ask themselves, "What if something goes wrong?" They prepare for the worst case scenario and focus almost exclusively on preventing its occurrence. Many of you have become experts at implementing policies and procedures that prevent misconduct and costly mistakes.

But, this strategy usually ends up squashing the good outcomes as well as the bad, greatly limiting creativity, innovation, empowerment, employee engagement and trust.

I have a good friend who works for a large food manufacturing facility. The plant is located in a small Midwestern town that boasts of a labor force with a stellar work ethic. This particular employer has a strict "no fault" attendance policy which follows the progressive discipline model.

A no *fault attendance policy* is one in which employees earn points (often referred to as occurrences) for each work absence no matter what the reason for the absence may be.

Employees are allowed only a certain number of points before they will receive disciplinary actions for poor attendance.

My friend took his performance at work very seriously. For over five years he never missed a day of work. He often bragged about the time he worked a 12-hour shift with an untreated broken foot. He was the ideal employee earning the award for perfect attendance year after year.

...And then he had children.

As all parents know, babies get sick, often. My friend (whose wife also worked outside of the home) quickly received a verbal warning for work absences. Soon after, his infant son was hospitalized for pneumonia, and he was issued a written warning for missing another shift. He was told that the documentation of his offenses would be put in his permanent file. (This was corporate protocol.)

My friend has always prided himself on being a good employee. The thought of having a permanent reprimand in his file rocked him to the core. He instantly began to talk about finding a new job. His work suffered, and his co-workers told me that he was no longer very fun to be around.

This lasted for almost six months. And, although I am happy to report that my friend is still employed and performing well at the plant, he is keenly aware (8 years later) that the written warning remains in his record.

The other unfortunate side-effect to this employer's attendance policy is that many of the workers learned early on how to "play the system." They keep a running count of their *occurrences* and manage the intervals between absences. After 12 months, an occurrence will drop off their record, and the employees feel free to again miss a day at work.

Keep in mind these are the same employees that make up the town's labor force with the reputation of having an *outstanding work ethic*. These are not problem employees. Most of the staff considers the attendance policy to be an extension to their PTO (paid time off) benefits.

So how can we do things differently and get better results?

What would it look like if you started asking, "What if things go *right*?" What if you started looking at how you can influence your teams to move the ball down the field, instead of just making sure they are following the rules?"

What if we trusted our employees enough to revoke the attendance policy? What if everyone showed up for work and gained a greater sense of loyalty to the company? What if feeling trusted made them more productive?

I am often asked how to build better trust in organizations. I am sure that everyone expects me to offer a highly complex and complicated answer. But the best advice I can give to you is…

Hire people with good character; trust and treat them like adults, and they will act appropriately.

Now, I understand that there are one or two problem employees in every company, but hopefully they are in the minority. Stop trying to fix them (and eroding the trust of everyone else in the process). Get rid of them.

We can take a lesson from Plato, who philosophized: "Good people do not need laws to tell them to act responsibly, while bad people will find a way around the laws."

If you want to improve and win each and every game, you must run a good defense, but you must *also* implement an effective offensive strategy. You must provide the tools your team needs to win, coach them well, monitor the score and celebrate every victory.

Translation: winning leaders **invest** in the improved performance of every employee.

Always remember that if you invest well in your team, you will see great returns.

"When people really care about a cause, they will not only act on their own initiative, they'll move mountains to get the job done. Therefore, getting the word out, or communicating the need for change, becomes one of the most critical elements in inspiring others to follow. In all organizations, the difference between leaders and mere managers is understanding this basic principle."

- Donald T. Phillips
The Founding Fathers on Leadership
(Hatchette Book Group, 1997)

INVESTING WISELY

As any savvy investor knows, before jumping into the market, you are wise to research and analyze the investment options.

It is common sense to weigh the majority of your investment efforts toward traditionally high-performing accounts, which consistently deliver lucrative dividends. And, similar to a stock broker, your job as a manager is to maximize the return on your organization's human capital investments.

You have likely heard that most managers spend 80% of their time with the 20% worst performing employees. I have found this to be alarmingly true. Many leaders whom I encounter in my work consistently make poor choices about how to invest their time, effort and labor dollars. They are typically running ragged trying to turn around the "problem employees," and often neglecting the employees who are actually performing well.

I find that managers who are primarily focused on building a great defense rarely reach the end zone.

If you want to be wildly successful as a manger, you must invest wisely.

I highly recommend that you begin by conducting a full workforce analysis, in which you *quantify the value* and *forecast future dividends* of each and every team member.

Each position has a set of tasks, duties and outcomes that must be accomplished. When an employee performs the tasks and duties and achieves the expected outcomes, the return is *equal* to the investment made by the employer. Therefore, the value is zero. When an employee contributes beyond these general expectations, their *value*, therefore, increases.

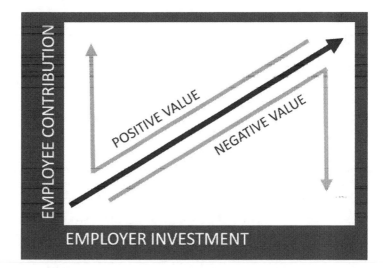

As you think about the value of each employee, you should calculate the associated investments. As the investments increase (wages, benefits, training, coaching time/effort, incentives, etc.), the return must also increase to maintain a positive value.

When coaching poor performers, I find that many managers want to give the employee "just one last chance." And, when I ask them how this will work, they often recount conversations about failed expectations and mistakes made. I hear about the issuance of well-meaning PIPs (performance improvement plans) in which employees are given 60-90 days to make improvements in their performance.

This approach seems noble and compassionate, but I think it is actually somewhat cruel. Unless these struggling employees are purposefully sabotaging their own performance (in which case they will welcome termination), they have more than fully proven to be the *least qualified* persons to determine how to improve performance. Employees like these need coaching (additional investment) from *you*.

So you must then ask yourself, "If I increase the investment in this employee, will this result in exponentially improved performance?" If the answer is yes, you need to get busy immediately implementing an in-depth coaching plan and monitoring for improved performance.

If the honest answer is no, you should do yourself *and* the employee the favor of termination. If additional investment in improved performance is ill-advised, then it is cruel to give the employee *one more chance* to fail yet again. The compassionate thing to do is help this employee find an opportunity in which success can be found.

Great leaders spend 80% of their time with the 20% highest-achieving employees. Everyone should have a *Performance Improvement Plan*!

Just like playing the stock market, increasing your investment in lucrative employees will deliver higher returns.

"True leadership rests in the understanding that people do not like being ordered around or told what to do. They would rather feel a part of the process, that their contributions really do make a difference, that they are part of a team rather than only a servant or an employee.

- Donald T. Phillips
The Founding Fathers on Leadership
(Hatchette Book Group, 1997)

BECAUSE THEY ARE NOT ROBOTS

In my HR career, I have worked with many leaders that I hold in very high regard. I have often seen some of these folks - whom I believe to be top notch in their field - almost melt under the pressure of being a manager. Although they are intelligent, dedicated and revered professionals, they will inevitably walk into my office one day and appear to be *broken*. Their hair is prematurely grey, their shoulders sag, their face is scrunched up in agony, and they will say to me, "What are we going to do with Bobby?" or, "Please help me with Sue." These managers have mastered the technical and mechanical components of their work, but managing employees is an entirely different monster.

This phenomenon has haunted and puzzled me for some time. So, a few years ago, I began asking the folks who attended my leadership development workshops this question: *Why is it so hard to manage employees?*

The best answer I ever got was, *"Because they are NOT Robots."*

I was awe-struck by how profound this simple statement was. Robots are predictable. We can program them to behave as we desire. They arrive with an instruction manual that explains how they work. We are trained how to fix them when they break. And, each one is similar - if not exactly the same - as the next. None of this is true of humans.

Although we can all agree that our modern workplaces vary greatly from the ones in which Frederick Winslow Taylor first implemented his management methods in 1911, the real dilemma lies in the fact that Taylor's management tools - which are still wildly prevalent today - are *highly logical*.

Logic is an incredibly valuable concept that is rampant in today's business community. We utilize logic in our accounting functions, pricing methods, inventory planning and many other business practices. However, when it comes to managing employees, a logical approach rarely yields the results we are looking for.

Let's explore. We are often told that when giving someone feedback, it is wise to sandwich the bad news between two positive comments. Sounds logical, right? Well, nine times out of 10, the employee will leave the conversation fixated on (and quite often derailed by) the bad news while having no recollection of the positive feedback.

I recently witnessed a performance review which provided 360 degree feedback to a highly capable CEO. (A 360 review is a process in which a professional's peers, customers and direct reports are asked to provide performance feedback to the leader - a very logical approach, right?)

Although 95% of the feedback given to the CEO was very flattering, 5% described ways in which the respondents thought she could improve her performance. This leader - who was usually fairly confident in her abilities - was crushed. She obsessed on the negative feedback for weeks, and her confidence - and performance - suffered. She logically agreed that the feedback was valid and helpful, but she could not get around the betrayal she felt.

So why is logic so useless when dealing with employees? Well, most neuropsychologists and behavioral scientists agree that *at least* 85% (some claim as high as 90%) of human behavior is driven by subconscious emotional triggers.

Often the human subconscious and emotions are completely absent of logical explanation; a fact of which many managers (and parents of most teenagers) are keenly aware. And in almost every situation in life, the needs of the subconscious inevitably win out over any logical endeavor our conscious may be focused on.

And, to further complicate this issue, the traditional management tools which we use every day (e.g., job descriptions, the annual review, progressive discipline, job titles, suggestions boxes, standard operating procedures, employee of the month programs, etc.) are all derivatives of this simple *logic-based* strategy:

> *Success will occur if the boss (who is in charge) makes the ultimate decisions of what, when, where and how the work will be done; incentivizes employees with the promise of rewards when they do well; and the threat of punishment when they don't.*

This ideology is often referred to as *command and control* leadership. This approach, which is the basis for operations in almost every American workplace today, has been proven to lead to improved performance in a surprisingly *narrow* set of circumstances.

As in Taylor's era, *command and control* is effective when the work being done is highly rudimentary and repetitive in nature. However, in the modern workplace, this type of work is often automated or outsourced.

The typical job today requires workers to excel at activities that require intellectual abilities such as: scrutiny, diplomacy, innovation, compromise, creativity, reasoning, conflict resolution, teamwork, perceptivity, speculation and a host of other highly complex skills. And unfortunately, in the modern workplace, this common approach of *carrots and sticks* actually restricts these abilities.

If you are managing *robots,* a logical command and control approach is a productive leadership model. But you now know that the behavior of *humans* is overwhelmingly driven by our subconscious and emotions.

I often meet leaders who take great pride in their ability to fully understand how to run, repair and maintain the machinery in their department to its highest efficiency.

However, many of these folks have little insight into what makes their employees tick.

I once met a supervisor who worked in a manufacturing facility. He realized that the equipment in his department was becoming more and more inefficient. His highly complex packaging machine was requiring a great deal of additional maintenance and repair, leading to increased expense and lost productivity. So, he decided to look into purchasing a new machine. He spent the next six months researching options and talking with vendors. After which he spent months analyzing the return on investment for the new equipment.

Subsequently, he spent nearly a year developing a strategic implementation plan. However, when he needed a new engineer to oversee the installation and utilization of the machine, he reviewed a pile of resumes, conducted three 60-minute interviews and hired a guy within a week.

On his first day the new engineer spent three hours in HR filling out paperwork (which they called new-hire orientation) and then went to work.

If your #1 responsibility as a leader is to ensure the success of others, you must conduct as much (if not more) due diligence on your greatest investment - your employees - as the packaging supervisor did with his new machinery. Therefore, since your employees are human (not robots) we must seek to better understand human behavior and the functionality of the brain in the workplace.

I have found that good leaders clearly understand the individual motivators, emotional responses and subconscious thought processes of each employee - Great leaders leverage these psychological triggers to improve employee performance.

I have entitled this scientific approach *Employee Psychology*. **No wait, do not close this book.**

I have conducted many leadership seminars and I have found that when I introduce the idea of *Employee Psychology* many in the crowd often become visibly uncomfortable. I will see folks start to check their

Employee Psychology: the practice of utilizing human nature and behavioral science methodologies to achieve greater

wristwatches and search for the closest exit. If I could read their minds, I am sure I would hear concerns like, *"Oh crap, she is gonna go Dr. Phil on us,"* or, *"I am out of here if she tries to make us talk about our feelings."*

I blame the '80s. (Now don't get me wrong, I loved the '80s. MTV, big hair, Trivial Pursuit, leg warmers, Bon Jovi... I loved it all!) But, during the '80s the business community sent us very clear messages about work.

We were told that if you want to be successful in your job, you need to hide your emotions. We heard things like, *"Don't take it personal, this is just business,"* or, *"Don't bring your personal problems to work,"* or (my favorite), *"Crying is a sign of weakness."* We were told to separate our work from our personal lives and that you need to be *"tough to make it in this business."*

Many of these ideals are still threaded into the modern work culture. Therefore, when I use the word *psychology* in reference to leadership, it tends to make folks squeamish.

But I have determined that all humans - whether we like it or not; whether we admit it or not; whether we talk about it or not - are primarily driven by our subconscious emotional motivations - even at work.

I have done the research, and I can attest that there is no off button that we can push to deactivate the *human stuff* that differentiates us from the robots.

So, as managers and leaders it does not make sense to ask your employees to suppress or hide their human tendencies. It is in your best interest to leverage our human factors to actually drive performance. This is the essence of employee psychology: t*o embrace and leverage human nature in a way that results in improved performance.*

In order to help leaders embrace and leverage their employees' subconscious triggers, I have developed the Emotional Performance Model.

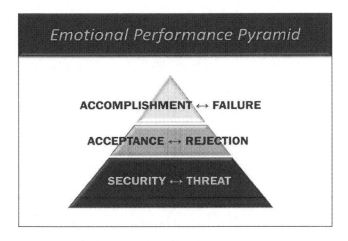

This pyramid outlines the dichotomy of emotions that impact the performance of every team member.

The **first level** represents the struggle between our sense of *threat and security*. We have all heard about the subconscious fight or flight response. This is our brain's physiological reaction to any perceived threat.

When our brain senses danger, it triggers our adrenal system to release the hormones cortisol and adrenalin. This hormonal cocktail physically and psychologically prepares us to either fight our enemy or flee from danger.

Because They Are not Robots 49

When our ancestors lived in caves, the fight or flight response was essential to survival. Every day they faced many life-threatening situations. Every moment was spent ensuring the availability of an adequate food supply, protecting the tribe from enemy attacks, fighting off ravenous animals and competing for a suitable mate. During this time our ancestors' brains were smaller than that of modern-day humans. As we have evolved through the generations our brains have expanded to allow for the onset of our complex intellectual functions such as reasoning, planning and analytical capabilities.

However, when we are in the throes of a threat response, our advanced intellectual functionalities all but shut down. Our primal instincts kick in, and our subconscious takes over. We become less capable of analyzing and categorizing the true *logical* level of a threat. Therefore, all threats (great and small; real and perceived) trigger the same physiological response.

For example, an employee that believes a co-worker is sabotaging her efforts will have the same adrenal response as a driver being carjacked at gun point.

As a leader, it is critical for you to understand that our subconscious has a voice. This is the little man (or little woman) that sits on our shoulder and looks out for our safety. I have named mine *Eddie Haskell.*

Eddie's job is to prepare me for all possible dangers. He instructs me to be on the look-out and responds when he sees an approaching threat.

And, Eddie likes stories. If he does not have all of the information to complete the story, he will finish writing the tale himself. And, Eddie does not work for Harlequin; Eddie idolizes Stephen King. Eddie will concoct stories of epic doomsday because his job is to prepare me to survive in the worst-of-the-worst case scenarios.

Let's explore this... Pretend with me for a moment that you have just checked your e-mail, and there is a message from your boss. It states that she and *her boss* need to meet with you right away.

What are you feeling? What are you thinking?

More than likely your Eddie is telling you that you are in trouble. You are probably racking your memory trying to figure out what you did wrong. I bet you are starting to think of all the ways that your boss has failed to provide you with what you need to perform (fight), or you are composing a list of the other companies in the area that could use your expertise (flight). Eddie is preparing you to survive the approaching tsunami.

I highly doubt that your Eddie said anything remotely close to, "Get ready my friend; you are being promoted," or better yet, "You're finally getting that raise you deserve."

Why would he? Preparing us for the good things in life is *not* Eddie's job.

So, as a manager, it is beneficial for you to understand and anticipate the threat response. Your main job is to improve performance, and the threatened human brain is rarely concerned about doing good work.

Our logic-based management systems are established on the precept that employees will improve when told that noncompliance will result in punishment (up to and including termination).

It seems only *logical* that a reprimanded employee will focus on improving his/her efforts. However, the converse is usually true. The threatened brain obsessively focuses on fighting or fleeing, which almost never results in improved performance.

So what can you do to promote security and minimize perceived threats? There are a few tactics...

First, emphasize clarity! Humans are naturally anxious about the future (thanks to Eddie's continual warnings). And, when we are uncertain of things to come, Eddie has a heyday. So, as a leader it is your responsibility to paint an incredibly vivid picture of the journey ahead.

Even if the picture is not entirely pretty, "Clarity," as Marcus Buckingham so eloquently noted in the book *The One Thing You Need to Know* (Free Press, 2005), "is the antidote to anxiety."

Second, utilize natural feedback when coaching. Often, when I observe well-meaning managers who are coaching a wayward employee, they generally provide feedback about how he or she has not met the *manager's* expectations. This approach establishes the manager in a position of *judge and jury.*

The manager decides what is considered *good* performance and what is essentially deemed *not-good* performance. Therefore when the employee experiences the threat response (which is almost inevitable in this situation), Eddie will communicate that the true enemy here is the *manager.*

Natural feedback is the ultimate outcome of performance. Good or bad, it is the fruits of our labor, the outcomes of our efforts.

Natural feedback sounds like this: "We missed our goal of landing five new clients," or, "Our waste increased 2% this month," or, "We've received four customer complaints this week." Although it is not always easy to hear, natural feedback helps Eddie target the *true* enemy - poor performance.

And, when you use the terms *us* and *we* it solidifies the manager as part of the solution instead of the object of conflict. And, you are then the perfect person to ask the question, "How do we fix this?" or, "How can we do better next time?"

The **middle tier** of the Emotional Performance Pyramid represents the subconscious dichotomy of *acceptance* and *rejection.*

Acceptance is one of the most powerful subconscious motivators. Eddie knows that we are herd animals and must live in tribes to survive.

I am always amazed when the news media covers a story about a child that has been locked away in an isolated cage. Although it is a sad story, it also teaches a great lesson about acceptance. These children have adequate air to breathe, they are given enough food and water to survive, but yet they do not thrive. They do not learn to walk or talk, and if left for an extended period of time without human contact, they actually die.

Acceptance in a peer group is an absolute *biological* need for all humans - especially at work.

Eddie knows that we belong to multiple tribes, our families, our communities, our clubs, our friends and our work team (among others). If you add up the hours you spend within each of these tribes, you will find that your *work tribe* is a very important part of your social existence. So, it is only natural that your employees would be subconsciously driven to seek acceptance within their work peer group.

And, this means that your tribe must always be cognizant of an invasion (or threat) from other tribes. You must band together against your enemies and protect each other from epic doom.

Now, we know that epic doom in the workplace is rare, but Eddie did not get the memo. If there is not a real threat from an opposing tribe, he will create one.

This is why Sales is always arguing with Operations, or the clinic folks don't work well with the hospital staff, or why the dayshift is forever competing against the nightshift.

I am a huge fan of the show Survivor (CBS). I find the show to be a microcosm of a human behavior lab that could not exist in the true scientific research community. And, although there are grand stories of betrayal, the loyalty that is generated in the first few days of the game is very telling about our human nature. Although the staffing of the tribes is random, the unlikely tribe mates form bonds that often last the duration of the show and beyond. Many winners have attributed their success to alliances that were established early and honored throughout the competition.

The same phenomenon happens in our workplaces. We seek out our tribe and become loyal to those who are loyal to us. Many of us establish workplace friendships that last long beyond our tenure at any company.

I met my best friend on day one of my first job out of college. We are now 20-some years older, and each of us has had many jobs in the interim. However, we are still as close as we were when we went to lunch during my initial orientation.

However, it was not until later in my career that I came to realize how close relationships can profoundly impact job performance.

I first met "Amy" when I interviewed for a position with a large corporation in Minnesota. After being hired as a Sr. HR Manager, I spent the first few months providing leadership development and upgrading the performance management program. I was soon asked by the CEO to partner with Amy to develop and facilitate an employee engagement training program for every supervisor and manager in the company (all 1200 of them).

For the next four months, Amy and I collaborated to develop a two-day training program to deliver to the organization. During this time I came to realize how much I admired Amy. Although our professional relationship introduced me to a new wealth of knowledge and techniques, it was our evolving friendship that encouraged me to explore strengths that I did not know I had.

Amy's confidence in me heavily outweighed that in which I had in myself. Her energy level and humorous outlook made the work feel like playtime. Business travel was not the drudgery it had once been; I actually looked forward to our trips together. And although we always worked very hard, it felt like we were being paid to go on vacation together.

We brought diverse talents to the project, but our personalities meshed graciously. This partnership was void of the judgment, resentment and competition I had experienced on many other projects. I never found myself questioning Amy's motives; I knew she had my back… and I had hers. We performed much better as a team than we could as individuals.

We accomplished things (including training *all* 1200 managers two months ahead of our goal) that we never imagined we were capable of. We received a great deal of praise and accolades for our work.

It was through this experience that I realized the unlikely magic of having a BFF-@-work. And, I soon realized that lightning can strike twice.

Our company was searching for a new HR expert to head up the Compensation and Benefits department. One of our co-workers suggested that we interview her mother who resided in Texas.

As soon as I met "Kate," I knew that she was overqualified for the job. But luckily, we hired her anyway.

Kate was in the later years of her career and looking forward to retirement, but she fit in with our team wonderfully. She was a self-proclaimed Southern Diva and I loved her outlook on life. She was proud and humble at the same time. She was confident and helpful all at once. And she may not have realized it, but Amy and I came to consider her our mentor.

Through her amazing ability to tell stories and relate her experience to our current situations, Kate provided profoundly impactful advice to both Amy and myself. She even taught us about the proper shoe choice of a true southern bell. (I can tell you that bright color, a four inch heel and an abundance of bling are crucial.)

We quickly became the *three* BFFs-@-work. This relationship helped each of us achieve heights of performance that we could not have accomplished without the support and encouragement of the other two.

Although Kate has since retired and Amy has moved on to a lucrative career training leaders all over the world, their friendship will continue to have an indelible impact on me as a professional woman (and diva wannabe).

As a leader you, will find that employees who feel accepted in the workplace will perform at a much higher level. I have a few ideas about how you can capitalize on this.

First, get out of the way. As a manager, you cannot force meaningful relationships to develop within your team, but you sure can prevent them. I am always puzzled when I hear about organizations that frown upon employees socializing. It is human nature to connect with people whom we spend a lot of time with, and to forbid such friendships in the workplace is futile.

I toured a manufacturing facility a few years back, and I was appalled by a recent policy they had implemented. They informed me that they were experiencing a serious decline in productivity and quality. Therefore, they had created a rule that you could only speak if you were standing on carpet. This meant that anyone on the concrete production floor (as opposed to the nicely carpeted office area) was bound to silence. The point was to encourage employees to focus on quality and productivity instead of socializing. Although their purpose was noble, the policy was incredibly misguided. Not only did quality and productivity continue to suffer, but they lost some of their best employees because they found the new policy to be totally degrading.

I recently heard a story about a gentleman who had been his girlfriend's supervisor for a number of years. They lived together and were parents of a toddler. I am told that both of these folks were highly valued employees until the day that they decided to get married. Their employer had a policy that you could not report to your spouse. They were told by the HR rep that one of them needed to resign or they would both be terminated.

Although these stories are extreme, I often find that employers do more to hamper workplace relationships than encourage productive ones; a fact that I find disturbing and highly counterproductive.

Second, you need to lead by example. Every workplace has its outcasts, bullies and wallflowers. Don't tolerate this within your team. Make sure that you are identifying and celebrating the strengths of each and every employee. Each person is unique and brings diversity to the team. If you accept each person as an integral member of the tribe, others will follow suit.

As the leader it is your responsibility to ensure that no one on your team feels rejected. Not only because it is the humane thing to do, but because it is extremely productive. Employees who feel like they are truly accepted for their unique qualities and are fully integrated into the group prove to be much more successful than those who are isolated.

Third, turn on the *Friday Night Lights.* Think back to high school. We all had fellow students whom we did not like or who did not like us. I remember a couple of girls that I did not care for simply because we were in competition for the affections of the same cute boy. And, girls of that age can be very catty.

However, on Friday nights during football season, we all wore the same jerseys and sat in the same bleachers.

I shared a sense of team spirit and school pride with the very same girls I had spent all week loathing. We cheered for our team together and sometimes even shot each other a high five. When the Friday Night Lights were on, we were united against a common enemy - the Urbandale High JayHawks (our arch rivals).

This sense of pride and team spirit can be very powerful in a work setting as well. As a manager you can foster this by identifying your arch rival: waste, or bad customer service, or your biggest competitor, or the threat of losing your best client (or whatever works for your team). Vilifying an external enemy can go a long way toward unifying a fragmented team. You may even want to pick team colors and invest in jerseys for casual Friday.

But keep in mind that as we grow and our circumstances change, our tribes may change as well. Just the other night I had a very enjoyable dinner with my college roommate, whom I had not seen in over 20 years, who also happens to be an Urbandale High JayHawks alum.

The **top of the pyramid** represents the dichotomy between a *sense of failure* and *feelings of accomplishment*.

Sometimes managers forget that humans have an innate desire to be a contributing member of a winning team. Who doesn't want to be the player that shoots the winning basket at the sound of the buzzer? Or, kick the winning field goal with two seconds left on the clock? Or, land a very lucrative account that the company has had their eye on for months?

Humans crave the prestige that comes from success. And conversely, we are petrified by the thought of being seen as a failure.

One of the fascinating things about human nature is that success begets success. The more accomplished someone feels, the more likely they are to achieve higher goals. So, as a manager it is in your best interest to help everyone gain a greater sense of pride and accomplishment.

How can you best do this?

First, focus on strengths. I work with many organizations that embrace competency-based talent development philosophies. In this strategy each position is analyzed to determine an exhaustive set of ideal competencies which are deemed necessary to achieve success in each unique role.

For example, the competency list for an operations manager will most likely include strong aptitude for:

- *problem-solving*
- *decision-making*
- *innovation*
- *forecasting*
- *communication*
- *strategic planning*

- *detail orientation*
- *process improvement*
- *data collection*
- *analytical thinking*
- *fiscal responsibility*
- *walking on water*

(Just kidding with that last one… kind of.)

In a competency-based system, every operations manager is evaluated on this exhaustive set of competencies. In the areas in which the manager does not excel (which is likely to be more than a few), we institute a *development plan* in order for the manager to work on his/her "areas of opportunity." And in a few months we will again assess the competencies to check for any performance improvement (or more likely - continued deficits).

Sound like fun?

Not to me. And, probably not to the operations manager.

This system continually highlights weaknesses, which enhances any employee's sense of failure and erodes his/her confidence. Whereas, focusing on strengths allows for greater achievement stemming from a firm sense of accomplishment.

I recently read about a study conducted at a reputable university. They wanted to test the theory that focusing on our innate strengths leads to greater achievement. So, they rounded up a group of volunteers and tested their reading speed. They separated the group into three categories based on the results: the slower readers, the average readers and the fast readers. The groups then participated in extensive training and a speed reading practicum, after which they were again tested. The slower group had a modest increase to their average reading speed. The average group saw no change in their rate of reading. However, the group that had the best initial results saw a tremendous increase in their reading speed.

The study concluded that if we focus our development efforts toward the areas in which we have the most natural talent, we are likely to see the greatest performance improvements.

In addition, research findings report that employees who have regular opportunities to focus on their strengths at work routinely achieve greater success on the job than their colleagues who are *not* regularly encouraged to focus on their strengths.

Second, keep score. In this day and age, society frowns on keeping score. Because we want everyone to feel valued, we are reluctant to differentiate winners and losers. Therefore, many managers make the mistake of awarding effort instead of results.

Although we want everyone to give their best, effort doesn't pay the bills. And, employees recognize this. They know when they have not been successful, and it is not productive for us to placate to them by congratulating their good effort.

It is human nature to compete and evaluate our performance against a benchmark. If you do not track metrics that reflect true outcomes, employees may become confused or complacent.

How can you win the game when you don't know the score?

It is wise to establish key performance indicators (points on the scoreboard) and acknowledge when someone falls short of the goal line. You should then ask how you can help the employee move the ball in the future.

If you do your due diligence to learn about how the human brain operates and you apply the concepts of employee psychology, you will inevitably see major improvements to individual, team and organizational performance.

You will also be less likely to come into my office with your shoulders sagging, your face scrunched up in agony and beg me to replace your entire workforce with robots.

"By being out front and taking people where they've never before been, leaders essentially act as agents of change. And yet, in what is a fundamental tendency of human nature, people often react emotionally, with trepidation and anxiety, when presented with an unknown future. Accordingly, the best leaders know that before great numbers of people can be moved to act, they first must be informed of facts and information regarding current affairs – and then persuaded as to why they should consider changing."

- Donald T. Phillips
The Founding Fathers on Leadership
(Hatchette Book Group, 1997)

SNOWFLAKES AND ZEBRA STRIPES

If you are like most leaders I meet, you have been told by numerous well-meaning Human Resource professionals that in order to excel you must be vigilantly consistent and treat each employee exactly the same.

You were probably also conditioned (likely by the same well-meaning HR folks) to believe that the greatest shame of all leaders is to be accused of *playing favorites.*

Well, get over it.

As most parents of more than one child, good teachers and great managers can tell you, when you are dealing with human beings, there is no *one-size-fits-all* approach that actually gets results.

As a parent of two beautiful boys, I learned this lesson early on. If there were a contest for the most differing personalities among siblings, my boys would take the blue ribbon, hands down. My older son is the perpetual rule follower. He craves structure and approaches tasks in a methodical and orderly manner. He is the first to read the rules for a new game and he follows the detailed instructions to the letter. He is brilliant and obedient at the same time.

My younger son, who amazes me with his insights and intuitiveness, is forever stretching the boundaries of his world. He likes to explore options and keep his toes just immediately shy of crossing the line. When faced with a new concept that he may not fully understand, he makes up his own set of rules about how the world must work. For example, if he sees that the winner of the race was wearing a blue shirt, he keenly decides that blue is a "winning color."

The difference in my boys became glaringly clear at Thanksgiving dinner when my youngest was three years old. During my older son's toddler years, we had great success with the time-out method. If he was doing anything inappropriate we would simply warn him that if he did not stop he would earn a time-out. This always resulted in immediate obedience. I don't recall that we ever actually issued a time-out; the mere thought of it was enough to change his behavior. So, assuming that this method was a parent's greatest treasure, we felt well-armed for the *terrible toddler* years of our second son... we could not have been more wrong.

This particular Thanksgiving dinner was an important one for me. As a young mom in a new house, I wanted to host the holiday for our family. I planned, and cooked, and fretted for days in advance. As the day approached, I set the table with my best dinnerware and my grandest fall centerpiece. I confirmed the attendance with all the relatives. I collaborated with my in-laws to rotate casserole dishes in and out of our ovens to ensure all of the fixings were done at the precise moment. I was ready!

As we all sat down to my elaborately planned meal, we started to pass the delicious bowls of holiday staples one-by-one around the table. As the giant dish of mashed potatoes came within reach of my three year old, he decided to be a comedian and took a fingerful of spuds and wiped it on his nose. He thought he was hilarious (and so did Uncle Ted). I, however, was less amused.

I softly leaned over and told my adorable toddler that if he did that again he could expect a time-out. I felt reassured that this would be the end of things. No harm done. The magic of time-out was my saving grace, right? Well, my lovely son looked at me for a moment, contemplated the decision, nabbed another fingerful of mashed potatoes, wiped it on his nose and proceeded to walk over to the corner to assume his time-out.

The lesson for me as a mother was the same lesson that I have learned as a manager. No two humans on the face of the earth are the same. If you are trying to teach, coach, encourage or influence human beings, you must adapt to the uniqueness of each *individual*.

As a social scientist, I am forever intrigued by the "nature vs. nurture" debate. I love to study the varying opinions about the level of influence that genetics, brain science, upbringing, life experiences and environment have on human behavior. However, I have not landed firmly in either the nurture or nature camp. Because, when looking at leading employees (my true passion), neither nature nor nurture matters… we are each wonderfully unique.

To validate my point, I once reached out to a manager who supervised identical twins. These two individuals shared both nature and nurture. However, when I spoke with this manager I learned that she managed these folks very differently. One of the twins really liked to have direct daily contact with the manager and enjoyed starting his day with a conversation about the tasks at hand. The other twin was much more introverted and preferred to communicate through e-mail. This gentleman responded really well to written guidance and feedback.

As a manager, because you have no input into the nature or nurture of your team members, it is imperative that you dig in and learn about the unique personality traits of each individual. Like snowflakes and the stripes on a zebra, every person is wonderfully different from the next. If you want to be a great leader, you will make an effort to understand the unique nuances of each individual you work with.

One of the most important insights you can possess about your team members is the manner in which they process information, generate ideas and make decisions.

Take me for example: I truly enjoy sitting down and discussing all the variables and possible solutions to each and every situation. I love to explorer the "what if" outcomes of all the possibilities. Only after a very in-depth look into my crystal ball can I express why I prefer any one particular idea over the others. However, I can be easily influenced to change my mind by the thoughtful and/or provocative ideas of someone I trust and admire.

Through the years I have been labeled as "flighty," "having my head in the clouds," and "unfocused." However, this style works best for me. My personality demands that I engage in intellectual conversations and explore progressive ideas before I can develop a strategy that usually proves to be the right decision for me.

My husband, on the other hand, has a very different approach to decision making. I call him "the noodler." (Which, by the way, is a great name for a villain in the next Batman movie, don't you think?) Whenever he is faced with a decision, he needs to research the issue, gather all related information, consult with all parties and then spend a considerable amount of time reflecting on the possibilities. Once he has come to a conclusion, he will then step forward and announce his position. I learned long ago that once he has landed, I am just wasting my time by trying to engage him in a negotiation (as I so love to do); his mind is usually set.

Although, after 10+ years of marriage, my husband and I have adapted to each other's varied style, differences like these in the workplace can derail a team. You need to take the initiative to identify, accept and leverage each team member's personality. If you embrace and account for each individual's uniqueness, the team will follow. Then - and only then - you can unleash their greatest potential.

There are many aspects of individual personality that you need to discover about each team member. Such as: the way in which they learn best, their career interests and aspirations (I call those occupassions), their strengths and weaknesses, their communication style, whether they are a "meticulous planner" or a "habitual procrastinator" (both of which - by the way - can be very effective work styles) and most importantly, you need to fully understand what they expect from you.

"Leadership should be born out of the understanding of the needs of those who would be affected by it."

~Marian Anderson

WHAT GOT YOU HERE
WON'T GET YOU THERE

When I talk with leaders and mangers, I really enjoy hearing about their success stories. I often ask them to highlight their greatest career accomplishments. Frequently, I hear about exhaustive efforts to standardize procedures, improve processes, meet regulatory requirements or getting back to the functional basics.

The focus on process and efficiency has been a trend in all industries for the past three decades. Organizations such as

McDonalds pride themselves on the fact that a hamburger prepared in New Jersey will taste exactly the same as one ordered in New Mexico. Consultants across the globe have capitalized on the fad of aiding companies to become ISO certified. And, *Six Sigma, Lean Manufacturing* and *Just in Time Inventory* projects are all still popular strategies.

When I conduct organizational needs analyses for employers, I usually scrutinize their employee development efforts. Regularly the training plans focus strongly on technical functionality, policy adherence, regulatory compliance and procedural guidelines. Often new employees are paired with a veteran team member who has been given instructions to teach the rookie about the *nuts and bolts* of the job.

However, when I ask leaders about the challenges facing them in the near future, I rarely hear concerns about process or efficiency. Most of the time, they express their anxieties about failing to relate to customers, poor teamwork (often referred to as the silo effect), disrespect amongst employees, lack of trust for management, negativity or turnover.

Success in the modern workplace is dependent upon everyone's ability to cultivate and maintain quality relationships. Although we still need to have solid processes in place, winning or losing is highly impacted by how we connect interpersonally with all stakeholders.

Most of today's jobs require us to work alongside others the majority of the time. We can have the best protocols in place, but if we can't relate to customers and colleagues, success is farfetched.

As a leader, it is critical that you understand the important role that relationships play in your organization. It is imperative that you put just as much (if not more) effort into developing strong relationships as you do for improving processes.

It is your responsibility to ensure that your team also has the skills necessary to build quality relationships. Unfortunately, there is no formula or procedure that we can employ to ensure the cultivation of the lasting relationships we need.

Even HR - the department that is supposed to have a good handle on relationship building - struggles with this concept. Most HR professionals have spent countless hours trying to develop a *system* (or process) around building relationships. We are endlessly searching for the perfect orientation check-list, the best coaching script or the latest feedback forms.

I was once working with a CEO who truly understood the power of quality relationships. He was very dedicated to the idea of connecting with his team and his colleagues. However, in one of our early coaching sessions, he insisted that I provide him with a template for building these relationships. He was so accustomed to the *systematization* of leadership that he was unsure how to proceed without the proper forms, instructions or checklists. When I told him that there is no relationship building formula to follow, he became frustrated and struggled to move forward.

Think about the quality relationships in your life: your spouse, your parents, your children, your neighbors, your siblings, your friends. Could you develop a template for how these relationships are built and maintained? Can you write a script for being a great friend? Can you make a checklist for being a helpful neighbor? Is there a formula for a successful marriage? Of course not; because there is no standard operating procedure for building quality relationships.

Highly successful organizations that realize the importance of relationships spend a great deal of time (and money) to ensure that their employees possess the skills needed to develop, and leverage professional relationships. They provide training and coaching opportunities that focus on communication, conflict resolution, negotiation, networking and many other important interpersonal skills.

I highly encourage you to analyze your approach. Do you emphasize the need for quality relationships? Do you provide your team with the support and training they need to nurture their professional relationships? If not, you are limiting your potential. You and your team will achieve much greater results when you can forge a balance between process and relationships.

"Leadership is not so much about technique and methods as it is about opening the heart. Leadership is about inspiration—of oneself and of others. Great leadership is about human experiences, not processes. Leadership is not a formula or a program, it is a human activity that comes from the heart and considers the hearts of others. It is an attitude, not a routine."

—— Lance Secretan,
Industry Week, October 12, 1998

US vs. THEM

When working with leaders and teams, I am always concerned when I hear folks talk about an "us vs. them" culture. I am keenly aware of how this phenomenon erodes trust and achievement in any organization.

A few years ago I was facilitating a leadership development program for a large corporation. I conducted many sessions across the country with the management staff. The program was focused on creating a work environment that empowered the managers and engaged employees to deliver on the company's brand promises. I was encouraging managers to take initiative and challenge the status quo. However, in almost every session, someone would interject and explain, "They will never let us do that." The resistance to the message was palpable. You could sense their fear and trepidation as they spoke about *them* and how *they* would respond to the progressive strategies we were exploring.

But when I asked, "Who are *they*?" I would get responses like: *the executive team, senior leadership* or the *top bosses*. However, no one could ever give me a specific name. And I found this a bit perplexing because it was essentially the executive team that had commissioned me to deliver this new message. It was on their command that we were embarking on this culture change journey.

The whole experience reminded me of the B-movie *The Hills Have Eyes* (1977, Wes Craven). The film depicts a family that is stranded in the desert and being tormented by an unseen enemy that lurks just beyond the sand dunes. Although the enemy never actually appears on screen, the audience is keenly aware of the danger *they* pose. This is a particularly effective cinematic technique. Products of the human imagination are much scarier than any creature Hollywood can dream up. Fear of the unknown is a greater threat than any monster ever confronted.

As I worked with more companies, I realized that *us vs. them* is a workplace epidemic. This problem exists to some degree in almost every workplace I have studied.

Recently, I began to take a closer look to try to dissect this issue. Initially I anticipated that I would uncover vast leadership deficiencies. I theorized that overbearing bosses were most likely the catalyst to this trend. But, I was wrong. I found that even teams who really like their supervisors tend to believe that someone (or some group) in their organization should be viewed as an antagonist. They believe that *they* have ulterior motives and will inevitably make decisions that are harmful to *us*.

So if this is a common occurrence in most organizations, how can you transcend this issue? In your company, you can start by acknowledging that the problem is not necessarily caused by the *people* in the situation; it is driven more by the *structure* of the relationships.

The concept of a reporting structure (or chain of command) automatically establishes an organizational pecking order. And human nature drives us to subconsciously fight to climb the totem pole. Even if we adore our boss, the fact that they have authority over us (and we are in a subordinate role) creates a parent-child dynamic. These relationships will always be overshadowed by an imbalance of power. The boss has the ultimate say over the employee's continued employment, career advancements and compensation. This fact alone prevents a level playing field and erodes trust - no matter how great the boss is.

I believe that we must first address this issue by redefining the role of the manager.

The most important (and I assert the only) metric that should measure managerial performance is the level of success achieved by his/her team members. Every manager should evaluate his/her own performance in direct correlation to the performance of those they are coaching. If the employee is failing - the manager is also failing. If the employee is excelling - the manager is excelling. The manager's continued employment, career advancement and compensation should directly reflect that of the team members. This allows for the parent-child dynamic to evolve into a true partner-based relationship.

I am currently coaching a manager (we will call her Tammy) who has had difficulty connecting with her staff. She has worked in the facility for over 25 years, as have many on her team. When I was talking with the employees to gain insights into their team dynamic, most had a similar perspective. They told me that when Tammy was their co-worker she was friendly and helpful. They all enjoyed working alongside her for many years. But when she was promoted, she changed. They told about how she became cold and hardnosed. They described her style as "overbearing" and stopped relying on her expertise.

Tammy's story is unfortunately a common one. Many new managers believe that the promotion requires them to change how they behave at work. They were once told (and believed) that if you want to be a successful manager, you can no longer be friends with your employees.

When I ask new managers why they believe they need to distance themselves from the employees I usually hear, "Because I may need to fire one someday." And, although this is a true statement, the more accurate assessment is:

> *You will probably fire a handful of people during your management tenure. However, the multitudes of employees that you won't need to fire will highly benefit from a meaningful relationship with you.*

The best advice I can give to new managers is to be *truly authentic* in your role as a manager. Don't try to be someone that you are not. You were promoted to a management position because you have qualities that set you apart. Embrace those unique qualities and be true to your personality.

Some of the most effective leaders I know make a point to showcase their vulnerabilities. They are human and they are not afraid to show it. Humans make mistakes and do dumb things... own it. Authenticity will earn you great respect and loyalty from your team.

I am a very clumsy person by nature. I am forever doing things that would greatly embarrass most speakers. I am a very animated presenter; I pace frantically, talk with my hands, and wave my arms erratically. I have tripped over cords while training, and I have even broken a heel on my shoe during a particularly active session. However, I realized the value of owning your imperfections in one life-changing moment...

I was in a smaller training session with about 25 top leaders of a client I was working with. I had been delivering my high-energy *mojo* for about two hours when a gentleman in the first row motioned for me to lean down so he could whisper in my ear. He then changed my life by telling me, "Ma'am, you should know that your fly is open."

I had two options: I could run and hide in total humiliation, or I could own it. I chose to own it, and I announced to the entire group that I would finish the presentation with my fly firmly closed.

This level of vulnerability (and humor) allowed me to connect with this group of people in a way that no amount of planning or expertise could bring. They saw me as just like them: a truly flawed human just trying to do my best despite adversity.

So many leaders believe that you gain respect and reverence by demonstrating the utmost professionalism at all times. I believe this is too tall of an order for even the best leaders. None of us are perfect, and we lose credibility if we pretend that we are.

"Confronted with a doctorial situation in corporate America, for instance, people may not openly say what's on their minds, but they will speak to each other about their feelings. Whispers in the hallway, in the restrooms and in the cafeteria may become part of a larger rumor mill until perception becomes reality in the minds of many employees- until they become followers no more."

- Donald T. Phillips
The Founding Father on Leadership
(Hatchette Book Group, 1997)

EMPLOYEES ARE YOUR GREATEST INVESTMENT

The Gallup Corporation has spent many years researching effective leadership. They have become the pinnacle experts on the subject of effective management techniques. The book *First Break All the Rules* (Marcus Buckingham and Curt Coffman, Gallup Press, 1999) first introduced the world to the merits of focusing on employee engagement.

Employee engagement is defined as the positive (or negative) emotional connection to the work we do, which in turn drives (or inhibits) real business results. If an employee is fully engaged, they are much more likely to deliver higher productivity, greater customer loyalty, better workplace safety and stay longer with your company than their disengaged peers.

For the last 15 years, many companies across the US and the world have realized that in order to compete in our ever-changing markets we need not only have the best and brightest on our staff, we also need to ensure that our best and brightest are fully engaged. The concept of employee engagement has become common rhetoric in business plans and human resource strategies around the globe.

However, although many organizations have seen steadily increasing employee engagement survey scores, they have not yet realized the correlating improved business results they had anticipated.

I applaud any organization that is focused on improving their employee engagement. After much reflection and research, I have concluded that employee engagement is *still* a key component to sustainable success in any organization.

But, if your current efforts are not impacting your bottom-line, you may have fallen victim of one (or all) of the four common mistakes organizations typically make when implementing employee engagement initiatives.

First, I have found that many well-intending organizations mistakenly associate employee engagement with job satisfaction. Although job satisfaction may promote fleeting spikes in talent retention, it rarely leads to sustainable bottom-line improvements.

Often these organizations will conduct elaborate engagement surveys and then bring teams of employees together to discuss the results. These teams are called upon to develop action plans to help improve the scores for the next survey.

I understand the desire to include employees in this process, but most members of these teams are not trained in the intricacies of human behavior or the detailed aspects of employee engagement. Their understandably biased perspective is geared toward providing better job perks and work conditions. So although the outcomes of these teams are well intended (and may temporarily boost job satisfaction), they are rarely effective at driving *true employee engagement.*

Secondly, I have found that many organizations have an inflated view of the importance of the engagement survey itself. The survey is an imperfect tool. Unless you were to send all of your employees to a neuropsychological diagnostic lab, the results reported on your employee surveys are subject to many contradictory influences and errors.

The survey, although a helpful tool, is not the end-all-be-all that some leaders make it out to be. I often liken it to the experience of encountering a sick child.

When a child approaches us and states, "I do not feel good," our usual response is to put our hand on the child's forehead or fetch a thermometer to take the lad's temperature. The act of checking the temperature gives us a little bit of information - just enough to determine what to do next. If the forehead feels hot, we may ask the child if his/her tummy hurts. Or if the thermometer reads 100.1, we may reach for a cold compress.

However, checking the child's temperature alone does not provide a diagnosis, nor does it cure the ailment. Similarly, the employee survey is just an indication of the current engagement temperature of your employees.

Third, many leaders look at the survey score as a reflection of their own success. They believe that if their engagement survey scores are increasing they must be doing a good job. This is a dangerous perspective. Your customers do not pay you for rising employee engagement scores.

Your customers want high-quality products and services at a reasonable price. In order to deliver, you must ensure that your staff is physically, emotionally and intellectually invested in delivering high-quality products and services in the most efficient manner (i.e., fully engaged).

Employee engagement is not a goal, it is a *strategy*.

Often, considering survey scores as an indicator of manager performance will lead to inaccurate survey data in the future. It is human nature to want to be viewed in a positive light, so managers will inadvertently start to manage to the survey score. They will (usually unknowingly) influence their employees to respond more positively on subsequent surveys. This will lead to better scores, but rarely impacts *true engagement* (the emotional connection to the work), which is what drives improved performance (which is the real goal).

Lastly, I have come to realize that focusing on engagement without promoting accountability is a flawed recipe and usually leads to widely spreading levels of employee entitlement. It is important for employees to emotionally connect with the organization, their team and the work they are doing. But without personal accountability, it is unlikely that employees will continually strive to deliver their best and seek out ways to achieve their highest potential.

I first encountered this problem while working with a mid-size employer. I connected with the administration team, and for months we strategized about developing an environment that fostered engagement. We surveyed the employees, met with each team and instituted what we believed to be highly positive changes. However as we moved forward, I realized that the team members were becoming more and more pessimistic about the impact of the project. Team discussions would quickly spiral into explanations of how management was not doing enough to make things better. When asked for input, the employees started calling for things like additional vacation hours, better compensation, new schedules, less responsibility and additional staff. And although we understood their desires, we knew that fulfilling these requests would not increase engagement and would likely hamper progress toward our goals of providing higher quality services and growing the organization.

I soon realized the missing element in our program was *personal accountability*. The employees had difficulty understanding how their personal situations related to the sustainability and success of the organization as a whole.

This increased level of entitlement became a large obstacle for the administration and we inevitably had to step back and regroup.

I learned long ago that leaders will readily consider new ideas, but if I want them to embrace and implement new techniques, I need to provide them with valuable tools and resources.

So, I will conclude this book with six practical management strategies that you can deploy tomorrow to increase employee engagement and promote personal accountability within your team.

Performance Descriptions

Many managers and HR professionals invest countless hours of blood, sweat and tears developing complex job descriptions.

These documents usually comprise a list of required tasks to be completed and are often accompanied by numerous standard operating procedures. A job description is a good tool to outline tasks, duties, physical requirements, essential functions and reporting structure of the job; however, it fails to paint a vivid picture of what top performance really looks like.

So, I think we should redirect our energy towards developing *performance descriptions*. This is less of an instructional document and more of a guideline for defining good, great and poor performance. If we have quantifiable definitions of performance, then we can truly evaluate the *VALUE* of our greatest investments.

A few years ago I was conducting an interview for a senior management role in a marketing company. After giving the candidate a copy of the job description, he replied, "This is helpful, thank you. But, can you please describe the contributions of someone who you would consider to be highly effective in this role?"

I was shocked (and impressed) by this unusual question. What I realized in that moment is that we - as an organization - had restricted our view of performance. We had painstakingly described the minimum requirements for our employees. We had given each of them a formal document which clearly defined the steps they needed to take to be "good enough." But, we had not informed them of what it would take to be a *superstar* (which is what we were ultimately longing for).

When engaged in conversations with employees you need to clarify superstar performance expectations on two different - yet highly interconnected - levels: the *what* and the *how*.

The *what* conversation describes the outcomes of the role. What is the true purpose of this job? This is not a consideration of the person in this role; it is a true analysis of why we created the job in the first place. *What* was the original need? At the end of the day, *what* does this role need to accomplish for us to be truly successful?

I urge you to be careful when defining the *what*. It is very easy to fall into a discussion about deadlines, policies, processes and procedures. These are important parts of our day to day work, but highly effective employees will most likely uncover these things on their own. What they need from you, their coach, is to define the **outcomes** required for superstar level success.

Outcomes can be looked at as the "fruits of our labor." Whereas the tasks and duties are the actual labor - the outcomes are the fruit (the sweet stuff). Few of us jump for joy when the proper procedures are followed or the tasks are completed. However, we tend to celebrate wildly when we land a new client, or impress our customers, or discover a new formula. The outcomes are the "party" worthy moments that we work so hard to achieve.

The *how* of performance refers to character. Each person demonstrates a personal character (positive or negative), which collectively leads to an organizational character.

If you are familiar with the Enron story, you have witnessed how negative character can lead to epic organizational failure.

The *how* refers to behavior which is hopefully driven by a solid set of organizational values. These values should be ever present when you are recruiting, coaching and planning for the future.

Here's a tip... don't just hire a team member for their good skills, hire them for their good character.

When I ask managers to identify their superstars and describe what sets them apart, I regularly hear about those who accomplish amazing outcomes, but it is always accompanied with stories of demonstrably admirable character.

When discussing "problem" employees, managers often say things like, "She is a great nurse, *but* patients tell us that she isn't very friendly," or, "He is our good salesman, *but* he is rude to the administrative staff." Although these folks may be nailing the *what* of their jobs, their teammates rarely consider them to be superstars because they have neglected the *how* on their road to success.

When you are coaching employees, it is critical to ensure that everyone understands the *what* **and** the *how* of their respective role.

<u>Building Perseverance</u>

This past summer my husband and I took our two boys to Northern Minnesota for a weekend getaway. As I was checking us into the lodge, my husband came to me and proclaimed that the bag of snacks we had packed for the trip had come open and the contents were spilled all over the back seat of our vehicle. I quickly responded to him, "You should do something about that."

He smartly replied, "I am doing something about it, I am complaining to you."

Although this was a sample of my hubby's cute sense of humor, the interaction reminded me of how many workers deal with adversity in their jobs every day. Too many of your employees have been taught that the best way to solve a problem is to send it up the chain of command.

I often see managers continuously "running on the gerbil wheel." They are constantly scurrying to deal with *this problem* or *that crisis*. Managers are forever telling me about how their entire day was spent "fighting fires."

Dedicated managers are naturally driven to help others. They are instinctive problem solvers and are usually flattered when others approach them for advice. However, we must keep in mind that your most important responsibility is to drive the performance of others. Therefore, it is your job to prepare them to achieve greatness, no matter what the circumstances.

If an employee comes to you to explain a problem they are having, there are *two things* you should never do: *Do not* take ownership of the problem and seek a solution by yourself, and *do not* accept the problem as a reason to lower expectations.

Instead, use the opportunity to challenge the employee to persevere and adapt. There will always be obstacles in the way of success. You can bet that behind each solution lies yet another problem.

The best employees are empowered to overcome all of the obstacles they face. They must address adversity head on and implement creative solutions to move closer to the goal, no matter how hard it gets.

Value Statements

It is instinctive for most managers to continually evaluate (and give feedback about) the performance of each employee. However, the value statement works a little differently. In order to promote personal accountability, the employee is the owner of this process. They are responsible for composing their own value statement and presenting it to you, their coach. This is their opportunity to validate their performance and to quantify their own value.

Similar to a bank statement, the value statement outlines the employee's contributions (returns) to the team. It provides a forum for honest discussions about how he/she can improve in the future (dividends), and comfortably ask for your assistance and counsel.

Without the evaluation (and the perceived judgment that is provoked in traditional performance reviews), Eddie remains quiet, allowing for truly candid conversations about performance. These are the interactions between employees and managers that prove to actually have positive influences on performance and the desired outcomes.

Meaningful Conversations

So if you want to fulfill your management destiny and maximize the return on your human capital, you now realize you must make wise investments. And, the most valuable currency you have at your disposal is *meaningful conversations*.

If you want to gain the knowledge and insights to assist each individual in realizing his/her highest potential, you must take the time to engage in one-on-one conversations. Through these discussions you will not only gain insight about how to best *coach, motivate* and *train* each individual, you will cultivate relationships that actually drive improved performance.

Traditional conversations about performance are often reflective and one-sided. The supervisor sits down with an employee and summarizes his/her observances of the most recent past. The supervisor usually offers an evaluation and suggestions for improvement. The employee listens and often internalizes the dialogue as a personal judgment. This rarely leads to strong relationships or improved performance. This is a tragically lost opportunity.

The time spent engaging in conversations with employees about *future* performance is the currency for the highest yielding investments. Although past performance needs to be considered, if you focus entirely on analyzing what has already occurred, you have no chance to impact the future.

The best managers spend a great deal of time and energy talking with employees about the future. If you and the employees are partners working together to achieve common goals, it is wise to make sure you are working in consistent alignment.

In order to assist each employee in achieving their greatest potential, you need to connect with everyone personally, which requires *meaningful conversations*.

However, it is also occasionally your responsibility to provide an employee with feedback that they may be reluctant to hear.

It is necessary to discuss performance deficits and mistakes promptly, but it is important that you do so in a way that does not erode trust and the relationships you have built.

These tough conversations are difficult for even the most seasoned managers. However, it is critical for employees to clearly recognize the realities of every situation. All too often, we are unable or unwilling to face our own shortcomings. But, to quote Dr. Phil, "You cannot change what you do not acknowledge."

So every leader needs to master the art of *loving candor*. This is a manner of candidly exposing the reality of the situation while demonstrating an authentic desire to help remedy the problem.

Many compassionate managers avoid these conversations because they do not want to stir up negative feelings. However, I feel that providing honesty and unyielding support is the most compassionate thing you can do.

I have a friend that is highly talented and successful. He is wildly admired in his profession and is revered by the business community. However, I came to realize that many of his colleagues were growing frustrated with him because he was failing to follow through on his routine day-to-day commitments.

I would often hear others whisper behind his back about his growing lack of respect for the team. This really bothered me because I knew how dedicated he was to his work *and* his co-workers. So, I sat down with him to try to understand the situation. He informed me that he had taken on a new project that was consuming a large portion of his work time.

He was engrossed in this exciting work, and he admitted to leaving loose ends with his daily duties. However, he failed to recognize the effect that this was having on his teammates.

As we continued our conversation, I realized that it was my duty to inform him of the negative consequences of his behavior. I told him that I was incredibly excited that he was working on such an important project, but I informed him that others were starting to question his dedication to the team. I candidly expressed their concerns and offered to assist him with rebuilding the quickly eroding relationships.

Although I felt uncomfortable (it would have been much easier to just congratulate him and sit back to wait for his approaching train wreck), I cared enough about this fellow to be honest with him. And, the fact that I sincerely wanted to help actually strengthened our relationship.

During difficult conversations, it is very tempting for managers to monopolize the dialogue. Most of us clearly present the facts and are quick to offer our assessment and guidance. However, in order to leverage the opportunity for learning, you need to be highly inquisitive.

Asking probing questions is the best way to engage an employee's conscious brain (and not wake a sleeping Eddie). Questions are usually void of any judgment or accusation, therefore minimizing the threat response. This allows the employee to maintain full utilization of his/her analytical and logical reasoning functions.

Team Incentives

In the modern workplace, teamwork is an essential ingredient in the recipe for success. And, just like baking cookies, if you have all the right ingredients minus one, the whole batch is ruined.

Think about the last time you received lousy customer service. Do you remember the name of the employee? Probably not, but I bet you remember what company he worked for.

You are not likely to tell your neighbors how *Sam* stacked the eggs on top of your loaf of bread in the grocery sack, but you will complain and tell your friends not to shop at the *Corner Grocery Stop*.

Everyone's individual contributions are interlinked, which determines the success (or failure) of the team as a whole.

You win or lose as a team.

Many employees report to work with a "me" attitude, and often these are your superstars. They have decided that in order to be successful, they will focus on *just doing my job*. They have witnessed the poor performance of others, and in order to remain successful, they have developed an invisible cocoon to isolate them from the negative influences swirling around them. They ask to be left alone and try not to get involved with any conflict. This approach seems logical, but it is misguided.

If you were in a life raft, wouldn't you extend your hand in attempt to rescue the people who are drowning in the water around you? How can you be considered successful if others on your team are failing? A truly successful employee ensures that all other team members are successful as well. This is not only noble, it is lucrative.

I have recently worked with a medical center that had a lab on-site to process medical tests for the attached hospital. The hospital nursing staff and lab personnel rarely interacted with each other beyond the computer system that linked their functions. The nurses were very proud of the level of care and service they delivered to their patients; however, they routinely failed to communicate effectively with the lab about the needs of the patients they were serving. And, one day the inevitable happened; the lack of communication led to a system failure. The error was eventually caught and corrected, but the patient was not pleased.

Of course, the lab blamed nursing, and nursing blamed the lab. However, blame is not the issue; teamwork is. When I started to dig into finding a solution to the problem, I realized that the two departments were running separate races with separate finish lines. Both teams had goals that were focused around their isolated functions. Because they were meeting their individualized goals, neither team was focused on the needs of the other. Therefore, they both missed the bigger picture: patient safety and satisfaction.

As a leader you can greatly influence teamwork and alignment if you offer team incentives. Instead of rewarding the quarterback for throwing a perfect spiral (that may or may not be caught by the wide receiver), reward the entire team when they work together to score a touchdown. If each team member realizes that winning requires teamwork, they will all focus more on the scoring than their individual agendas.

So, you need to decide what you are trying to accomplish as a team and define success as a *group activity*.

According to renowned management consultant and author Peter Drucker;

> *"The leaders who work most effectively never say I. And that's not because they have trained themselves not to say I. They don't think I. They think we; they think team. They*

understand their job is to make the team function. They accept responsibility and don't sidestep it, but 'we' gets the credit... This is what creates trust, what enables you to get the task done. "

Praise and Recognition

I consider the quest for *effective* praise and recognition tactics to be the "holy grail" of the modern human resources industry. If you go to any book store, you will find endless volumes describing the 101 best ways to praise and recognize employees. And, I have tried most of them.

I have facilitated numerous employee engagement surveys in my career. Almost all of them have a section that asks about the employees' perceptions of the organization's efforts to praise and recognize their contributions. I have come to dub this the *tanker question.* Because on 99% of the surveys I have compiled, this question receives the most negative feedback. I have yet to come across an organization that scores well in this area.

A few years ago I was invited to consult with a business services company that was concerned about the results from their recent employee satisfaction survey. They had spent the last 12 months (and a considerably large amount of money) implementing what they considered to be a progressive praise and recognition program.

They had hosted many parties and conducted numerous prize drawings. However, they still "tanked" on the praise and recognition section of their survey.

Similarly, I recently met an HR executive who made a commitment to visit every employee's work station on Friday at 2 p.m. to pat each person on the back and thank them for the work they do. After a few short weeks, the break room became very crowded around 2 p.m. A few individuals remained at their desks because they treasured the interaction with their boss. However, many of the folks congregating in the lunch room expressed their annoyance at the executive's insincerity. They made comments like, "He has no idea what I do, so why does he waste my time by coming by to thank me each week."

Earlier in my career, I worked for a large organization that had around 35 human resource personnel. In order to express appreciation to our employees, every month our department would host *Friday Food Day*. (I am not sure why most of these events tend to happen on Fridays, but they do.)

Keep in mind I am what you might call a "foodie." (I love food - especially the free kind.) And, I would ensure that I was in the office for every Friday Food Day. Please don't misunderstand; this was not your typical potluck that every office randomly has. Friday Food Day was a revolving array of delicacies and Grandma's best recipes. In the morning you could find egg bakes, assorted fruit drinks and donuts glazed with maple frosting and sprinkles. Later in the morning you could waltz over to the Friday Food table and find popcorn, pretzels, and other snacks of all variations. By lunchtime the table became full of chicken wings, sub sandwiches, pizzas with all different toppings and every casserole imaginable (aka *hotdish* for the readers in Minnesota). And, by afternoon (my favorite time of Friday Food Day) out would come the brownies, cookies and bars. It was pure heaven!!!

But when I took my survey each year and I was asked if I felt praised and recognized for doing good work, I would answer "no."

I looked forward to each and every Friday Food Day, and I did not want this tradition to end. But, it had nothing to do with *my* contributions. It was fun, but it did not make *me* feel successful. And that is the real purpose for praise and recognition.

Although I highly encourage every company to plan parties and food days, I must caution you against believing that these events are good ways to praise and recognize your team members.

For each of us, there is a sensation that I call the *rockstar feeling*. It is the extreme pride and sense of accomplishment we feel when we win, complete a difficult project, solve a problem or perform beyond expectations. It is a sensation like no other, and it motivates us to keep improving.

This is where praise and recognition comes into play. Although we can surely generate the *rockstar feeling* for ourselves, it can be magnified (and validated) by external feedback. However, the form of the feedback is highly personalized.

Whereas one employee may be totally energized by a customer compliment, another may be embarrassed by it. One person may relish being employee of the month, and another may be annoyed by it. (Don't get me started on the pitfalls of an employee of the month program - that is a topic for a whole other book.)

As a leader you need to discover the fuel that lights each individual's *rockstar* fire. And this is not an easy task. If you sit down and have a conversation with employees and ask the question, "How do you prefer to be praised and recognized?" most employees will tell you that they would enjoy receiving gifts or a raise in pay.

But, I have yet to see the award of a gift card (even from the best restaurants) light anyone's *rockstar* fire. I have found that, for most people, the trigger is often obscure and unanticipated.

For me, I often find myself experiencing a *rockstar* moment when I am speaking to a group. When someone in the room slightly smiles at me while nodding their head in agreement to what I am saying, I become essentially transformed into my *rockstar* self. I feel as though this person has stood up and declared me to be the "smartest person on planet earth." I interpret the head nods to be a direct attempt to tell me, "You are the brightest, funniest and most thought provoking speaker I have ever heard." And not only does my head swell a bit, I actually perform better. The continued fueling of my *rockstar* fire reminds me that I was born to do this work and I can't wait to do it again.

No matter what your title is, if someone at work looks to you for guidance, then congratulations, you are a leader. Although it is an incredibly tough job, it is a very important one.

Hopefully, your hair is still full of its natural color, and you are not "broken" yet. I have written this book to ensure that you will stay that way. Although I cannot guarantee that your hair will not fade in time, it is my hope that you now possess the knowledge, tools and desire to make a CRITICAL LEADERSHIFT.

Become a Champion:

Organizational change is difficult and does not happen overnight.

 If you would like to learn more about implementing the Critical LeaderShift concepts at your workplace, please contact us:

IDEATION CONSULTING
www.ideation-consulting.com
507-217-9767
saranda@ideation-consulting.com

"Leadership must be based on goodwill. Goodwill does not mean posturing and, least of all, pandering to the mob. It means obvious and wholehearted commitment to helping followers. We are tired of leaders we fear, tired of leaders we love, and tired of leaders who let us take liberties with them. What we need for leaders are men of the heart who are so helpful that they, in effect, do away with the need of their jobs. But leaders like that are never out of a job, never out of followers. Strange as it sounds, great leaders gain authority by giving it away."

— Admiral James B. Stockdale

ACKNOWLEDGEMENTS

I would like to thank a long list of people who helped make this book possible.

I must start with my husband and partner, Todd. Thank you for standing by me, even when my ideas seemed crazy. You are the love of my life, and I am so proud to be your wife. You have provided me with the opportunity to *have it all*. We have great kids, we have built a wonderful home, and because of you, I am able to chase my dreams every day. It hasn't always been easy, but it has been worth it. I love you. I would like to acknowledge the two *very best* bosses I have ever encountered: Jon Alexander and Chad Hagen. These two individuals taught me everything I know about leadership through their grand example. Both of these gentlemen effectively blurred the lines between manager and friend. They taught me that strong leaders are compassionate and supportive. They challenged and encouraged me at every opportunity. I strive hard to grow their legacy by emulating their ideals every day.

To my Mother-in-Law and best friend, JoAnn, thank you. You are my role model, and you have helped me to be a better mother. I could not have done any of this without your patience, guidance and support.

To my big sister Sheila... thank you for taking such good care of me. You have always been my guardian angel, and you made many sacrifices to pave my way. While most other teenagers were embarrassed to be seen with their younger siblings, you took me under your wing and showed me the ropes. You have always made me feel safe and loved. I am so proud to be your little sister!

To my parents, thank you for Cookie Park, Crawdad Cove and homemade Christmas tree decorations.

You may call it karma, fate or shear randomness, but I believe people are divinely sent to intersect in our lives at the times in which we need them the most. To the countless friends and colleagues that have stood beside me during the good and bad times - you know who you are... *infinite gratitude*!

ABOUT THE AUTHOR

Sara Christiansen is the owner and CEO of Ideation Consulting, a human resource consulting firm based in Minnesota. Since starting Ideation Consulting in early 2008, Sara has grown to become a nationally recognized thought leader and highly-regarded speaker.

After earning her degree from Northwest Missouri State University, Sara's expertise has evolved during her 20+ years as a Human Resource professional. She has worked with all different industries in both the public and private sectors.

While providing human resource and organizational development consulting services to numerous clients, Sara has also devoted her efforts to many collaborative groups. She has administered projects for SMAFE (Southern Minnesota Association of Food and Ethanol Employers), the Minnesota Rural Employers Association, Twin Cities Human Resource Association and the MediSota Group. She has also been commissioned by countless SHRM (Society for Human Resource Management) chapters across the United States to deliver inspirational keynotes and engaging workshops.

Her most recent endeavor has included an expanded division of her company to focus solely on the healthcare industry: *Ideation Healthcare*. Sara works closely with other industry experts to develop HR and Business Development solutions designed specifically for healthcare organizations.

Sara attributes her success to many factors, but she is especially proud of her ability to identify and embrace opportunities. She finds that often opportunities arise from seemingly casual conversations. Sara says, "If you are courageous enough to put yourself out there and you make a point to talk with people about your passions, amazing opportunities will follow."

Sara lives in New Ulm, a quaint German town in Southern Minnesota. With her husband Todd, she and her two boys enjoy the rewards of their rural, mid-western lifestyle.

"This is my commandment: that you love one
another as I have loved you."

John 15:12